ELIJAH

&

ELISHA

1 Kings 17

Elijah Fed by Ravens

17 Now Elijah the Tishbite, of the people who were staying in Gilead, said to Ahab, "As the Lord the God of Israel lives, before Whom I stand, for sure there will be no rain or water on the grass in the early morning these years, except by my word." 2 And the word of the Lord came to him, saying, 3 "Leave here and turn east. Hide yourself by the river Cherith, east of the Jordan. 4 You will drink from the river. And I have told the ravens to bring food to you there." 5 So he went and did what he was told by the word of the Lord. He went and lived by the river Cherith, east of the Jordan. 6 The ravens brought him bread and meat in the morning and in the evening. And he drank from the river. 7 But after a while, the river dried up, because there was no rain in the land.

The Woman Whose Husband Had Died

8 Then the word of the Lord came to him, saying, 9 "Get up and go to Zarephath, which belongs to Sidon, and stay there. I have told a woman there, whose husband has died, to feed you." 10 So Elijah got up and went to Zarephath. When he came to the city gate, he saw a woman there gathering sticks. He called to her and said, "I ask of you, get me a little water in a jar, that I may drink." 11 As she was going to get it, he called to her, "I ask of you, bring me a piece of bread in your hand." 12 But she said, "As the Lord your God lives, I have no bread. I only have enough flour in the jar to fill a hand, and a little oil in the jar. See, I am gathering a few sticks so I may go in and make it ready for me and my son. Then we will eat it and

die." 13 Elijah said to her, "Have no fear. Go and do as you have said. But make me a little loaf of bread from it first, and bring it out to me. Then you may make one for yourself and for your son. 14 For the Lord God of Israel says, 'The jar of flour will not be used up. And the jar of oil will not be empty, until the day the Lord sends rain upon the earth.'" 15 So she went and did what Elijah said. And she and he and those of her house ate for many days. 16 The jar of flour was not used up, and the jar of oil did not become empty. It happened as was spoken by the word of the Lord through Elijah.

Elijah and the Woman's Son

17 After this the son of the woman who owned the house became sick. His sickness was so bad that there was no breath left in him. 18 So the woman said to Elijah, "What do I have to do with you, O man of God? You have come to me to have my sin be remembered, and to kill my son!" 19 He said to her, "Give me your son." Then he took him from her arms and carried him up to the room on the second floor where he stayed. And he laid him on his own bed. 20 He called to the Lord and said, "O Lord my God, have You brought trouble to the woman I am staying with, by making her son die?" 21 Then he lay upon the child three times and called to the Lord, saying, "O Lord my God, I pray to You. Let this child's life return to him." 22 The Lord heard the voice of Elijah. And the life of the child returned to him and he became strong again. 23 Elijah took the child and brought him down from the second floor into the house and gave him to his mother. He said, "See, your son is alive." 24 Then the woman said to Elijah, "Now I know that you are a man of God. Now I know that the word of the Lord in your mouth is truth."

1 Kings 18

Elijah's Word to Ahab

18 After many days, the word of the Lord came to Elijah, in the third year, saying, "Go show yourself to Ahab. And I will send rain upon the earth." 2 So Elijah went to show himself to Ahab. Now the time without food was very hard in Samaria. 3 And Ahab called Obadiah who was the boss over his house. (Now Obadiah had much fear of the Lord. 4 For when Jezebel destroyed the men who spoke for the Lord, Obadiah took 100 of these men and hid them by fifties in a cave. And he fed them with bread and water.) 5 Then Ahab said to Obadiah, "Go through the land to all the wells of water and to all the valleys. It may be that we will find grass and keep the horses and donkeys alive, and not lose some of the animals. 6 So they divided the land between them to pass through it. Ahab went one way by himself. And Obadiah went another way by himself. 7 As Obadiah was on the way, Elijah met him. Obadiah knew who he was, and fell on his face and said, "Is it you, my lord Elijah?" 8 He answered, "It is I. Go and tell your owner, 'See, Elijah is here.'" 9 Obadiah said, "What sin have I done? Why are you giving your servant into the hand of Ahab to be killed? 10 As the Lord your God lives, there is no nation where the king has not sent men to look for you. And when they said, 'He is not here,' he made the nation prove that they could not find you. 11 Now you are saying, 'Go, say to your owner, "See, Elijah is here." ' 12 And after I have left you, the Spirit of the Lord will carry you where I do not know. So I will go and tell Ahab, and he will not be able to find you. Then he will kill me. But I your servant have honored the Lord since I was young. 13 Have you not been told what I did

when Jezebel killed the men who spoke for the Lord? I hid 100 men of the Lord by fifties in a cave. And I gave them bread and water. 14 Now you are saying, 'Go and tell your owner, "See, Elijah is here."' He will kill me." 15 Elijah said, "As the Lord of All lives, before Whom I stand, I will show myself to Ahab today."

16 So Obadiah went to meet Ahab, and told him. And Ahab went to meet Elijah. 17 When he saw Elijah, Ahab said to him, "Is it you, the one who brings trouble to Israel?" 18 Elijah said, "I have not brought trouble to Israel. But you and your father's house have. Because you have turned away from the laws of the Lord, and have followed the false gods of Baal. 19 So now call together all Israel to me at Mount Carmel. And gather together 450 men who speak for Baal and 400 men who speak for the false goddess Asherah, who eat at Jezebel's table."

Elijah on Mount Carmel

20 So Ahab sent news among all the people of Israel. And he brought the men who speak for the false gods together at Mount Carmel. 21 Elijah came near all the people and said, "How long will you be divided between two ways of thinking? If the Lord is God, follow Him. But if Baal is God, then follow him." But the people did not answer him a word. 22 Then Elijah said to the people, "I am the only man left who speaks for God. But here are 450 men who speak for Baal. 23 Bring two bulls to us. Let them choose one bull for themselves and cut it up and put it on the wood. But put no fire under it. I will make the other bull ready and lay it on the wood. And I will put no fire under it. 24 Then you call on the name of your god, and I will call on the name of the Lord. The God Who

answers by fire, He is God." All the people answered and said, "That is a good idea."

25 So Elijah said to the men who spoke for Baal, "Choose one bull for yourselves and make it ready first. For there are many of you. Then call on the name of your god, but put no fire under it." 26 So they took the bull which was given to them and made it ready. Then they called on the name of Baal from morning until noon, saying, "O Baal, answer us." But there was no voice. No one answered. They jumped and danced around the altar they had made. 27 At noon Elijah made fun of them. He said, "Call out with a loud voice, for he is a god. It might be that he is in deep thought or has turned away. He could be away traveling. Or it may be that he is asleep and needs to have someone wake him." 28 So they cried with a loud voice. They cut themselves as they had done in the past, with swords and spears until blood poured out on them. 29 When noon passed, they cried out until the time for giving the evening gift. But there was no voice. No one answered. No one listened.

30 Then Elijah said to all the people, "Come near to me." So all the people came near to him. And he built again the altar of the Lord which had been torn down. 31 Then Elijah took twelve stones, by the number of the families of Jacob's sons. The word of the Lord had come to Jacob's sons, saying, "Israel will be your name." 32 With the stones he built an altar in the name of the Lord. And he made a ditch around the altar, big enough to hold twenty-two jars of seed. 33 Then he set the wood in place. He cut the bull in pieces and laid it on the wood. And he said, "Fill four jars with water and pour it on the burnt gift and on the wood." 34 Then he said, "Do it a second time." And they did it a second time. He said, "Do it a third time." And they did it a third time. 35 The water flowed around the altar, and

filled the ditch also. 36 Then the time came for giving the evening gift. Elijah the man who spoke for God came near and said, "O Lord, God of Abraham, Isaac and Israel, let it be known today that You are God in Israel. Let it be known that I am Your servant, and have done all these things at Your word. 37 Answer me, O Lord. Answer me so these people may know that You, O Lord, are God. Turn their hearts to You again." 38 Then the fire of the Lord fell. It burned up the burnt gift, the wood, the stones and the dust. And it picked up the water that was in the ditch. 39 All the people fell on their faces when they saw it. They said, "The Lord, He is God. The Lord, He is God." 40 Then Elijah said to them, "Take hold of the men who speak for Baal. Do not let one of them get away." So they took hold of them. And Elijah brought them down to the river Kishon, and killed them there.

The Rains Come

41 Then Elijah said to Ahab, "Go up, eat and drink. For there is the sound of much rain." 42 So Ahab went up to eat and drink. But Elijah went up to the top of Carmel. He got down on the ground and put his face between his knees. 43 And he said to his servant, "Go up now and look toward the sea." So he went up and looked and said, "There is nothing." Seven times Elijah said, "Go again." 44 The seventh time, he said, "I see a cloud as small as a man's hand coming up from the sea." Elijah said, "Go and tell Ahab, 'Make your war-wagon ready and go down, so that the rain does not stop you.'" 45 Soon the sky became black with clouds and wind, and there was much rain. And Ahab went to Jezreel. 46 Then the hand of the Lord was on Elijah. He pulled his clothing up under his belt and ran before Ahab to Jezreel.

Elijah Gets Away from Jezebel

19 Ahab told Jezebel all that Elijah had done. He told her how Elijah had killed with the sword all the men who spoke for Baal. 2 Then Jezebel sent news to Elijah, saying, "So may the gods do to me and even more, if I do not make your life as the life of one of them by this time tomorrow." 3 Elijah was afraid. He got up and ran for his life. When he came to Beersheba of Judah, he left his servant there. 4 But he himself traveled for a day into the desert. He came and sat down under a juniper tree. There he asked that he might die, saying, "It is enough now, O Lord. Take my life. For I am not better than my fathers." 5 When he lay down and slept under the juniper tree, an angel touched him. The angel said to him, "Get up and eat." 6 Then Elijah looked and saw by his head a loaf of bread made ready on hot stones, and a jar of water. So he ate and drank and lay down again. 7 The angel of the Lord came again a second time and touched him, and said, "Get up and eat. Because this traveling is too hard for you." 8 So he got up and ate and drank. And he went in the strength of that food forty days and forty nights to Horeb, the mountain of God.
9 He came to a cave, and stayed there. The word of the Lord came to him, and said, "What are you doing here, Elijah?" 10 Elijah said, "I have been very careful to serve the Lord, the God of All. For the people of Israel have turned away from Your agreement. They have torn down Your altars and have killed with the sword the men who speak for You. Only I am left, and they want to kill me."

God Speaks to Elijah

11 So the angel said, "Go and stand on the mountain before the Lord." And the Lord passed by. A strong wind tore through the mountains and broke the rocks in pieces before the Lord. But the Lord was not in the wind. After the wind the earth shook. But the Lord was not in the shaking of the earth. 12 After the earth shook, a fire came. But the Lord was not in the fire. And after the fire came a sound of gentle blowing. 13 When Elijah heard it, he put his coat over his face, and went out and stood at the opening of the hole. Then a voice came to him and said, "What are you doing here, Elijah?" 14 He said, "I have been very careful to serve the Lord, the God of All. For the people of Israel have turned away from Your agreement. They have torn down Your altars. And they have killed with the sword the men who speak for You. Only I am left, and they want to kill me."
15 The Lord said to him, "Go, return on your way to the desert of Damascus. When you get there, set apart Hazael to be the king of Syria. 16 Set apart Nimshi's son Jehu to be the king of Israel. And set apart Elisha the son of Shaphat of Abel-meholah to speak for God in your place. 17 Jehu will kill the one who gets away from the sword of Hazael. Elisha will kill the one who gets away from the sword of Jehu. 18 But I will leave 7,000 in Israel whose knees have not bowed down in front of Baal and whose mouths have not kissed him."

God Calls Elisha

19 So Elijah left there and found Elisha the son of Shaphat. Elisha was plowing with twenty-four bulls, and was with the last two. Elijah passed by him and

threw his coat on him. 20 And he left the bulls and ran after Elijah and said, "Let me kiss my father and mother. Then I will follow you." And Elijah said to him, "Return. For what have I done to you?" 21 So Elisha returned from following him. He took his two bulls and killed them. Then he boiled their flesh over a fire, burning the wood cross-pieces the bulls used to pull the load. And he gave the meat to the people, and they ate. Then Elisha got up and followed Elijah and served him.

The Lord Speaks to Ahaziah

1 Now Moab turned against Israel after the death of Ahab. 2 Ahaziah fell through the window of his second-floor room in Samaria, and lay sick. So he sent men with news, saying to them, "Go and ask Baalzebub the god of Ekron if I will get well again from this sickness." 3 But the angel of the Lord said to Elijah the Tishbite, "Get up and go meet the men sent from the king of Samaria. Say to them, 'Are you going to ask Baal-zebub the god of Ekron because there is no God in Israel?' 4 This is what the Lord says. 'You will not leave the bed on which you lie. You will die for sure.'" Then Elijah left.
5 When the men returned to Ahaziah, he said to them, "Why have you returned?" 6 They said, "A man came up to meet us. He said to us, 'Go and return to the king who sent you. Tell him, "This is what the Lord says. 'Are you asking Baal-zebub the god of Ekron because there is no God in Israel? So you will not leave the bed on which you lie. You will die for sure.'"'" 7 Ahaziah said to them, "What kind of man was he who came to meet you and said this to you?" 8 They answered, "He was a man with much hair. He wore a piece of leather around his body." Ahaziah said, "It is Elijah the Tishbite."
9 Then the king sent a captain with fifty of his men to take Elijah. The captain went up to him and saw Elijah sitting on the top of the hill. He said to him, "O man of God, the king says, 'Come down.'" 10 Elijah said to the captain of fifty men, "If I am a man of God, let fire come down from heaven and destroy you and your fifty men." Then fire came down from heaven and destroyed him and his fifty men. 11 So Ahaziah sent to him another captain with fifty men. The captain said to Elijah,

"O man of God, the king says, 'Be quick to come down.'" 12 Elijah answered them, "If I am a man of God, let fire come down from heaven and destroy you and your fifty men." Then the fire of God came down from heaven and destroyed him and his fifty men. 13 So Ahaziah sent to him a third captain with fifty men. When the third captain of fifty men went up, he came and put his face to the ground in front of Elijah. He begged him and said, "O man of God, I beg you. Let my life and the lives of these fifty servants of yours be of great worth in your eyes. 14 Fire came down from heaven and destroyed the first two captains with their armies of fifty. But now let my life be of great worth in your eyes." 15 The angel of the Lord said to Elijah, "Go down with him. Do not be afraid of him." So Elijah got up and went with him to the king. 16 Then Elijah said to Ahaziah, "This is what the Lord says. 'You have sent men to ask of Baal-zebub the god of Ekron. Is it because there is no God in Israel to ask of His Word? So now you will not leave the bed on which you lie. You will die for sure.'"

17 So Ahaziah died, just as the word of the Lord had said through Elijah. Because Ahaziah had no son, Jehoram his brother became king in his place, in the second year of Jehoram the son of Jehoshaphat, king of Judah. 18 Now the rest of the acts of Ahaziah, are they not written in the Book of the Chronicles of the Kings of Israel?

2 Kings 2

Elijah Is Taken Up to Heaven

2 When the Lord was about to take Elijah up to heaven by a wind-storm, Elijah and Elisha were on their way from Gilgal. 2 Elijah said to Elisha, "Stay here, I ask you. For the Lord has sent me as far as Bethel." But Elisha said, "As the Lord lives and as you yourself live, I will not leave you." So they went down to Bethel. 3 Then the sons of the men who spoke for God at Bethel came out to Elisha. They said to him, "Do you know that the Lord will take Elijah from you today?" And he said, "Yes, I know. Say no more." 4 Elijah said to him, "Elisha, I ask you to stay here. For the Lord has sent me to Jericho." But Elisha said, "As the Lord lives and as you yourself live, I will not leave you." So they came to Jericho. 5 The sons of the men who spoke for God at Jericho came to Elisha. They said to him, "Do you know that the Lord will take Elijah from you today?" And he answered, "Yes, I know. Say no more." 6 Then Elijah said to him, "I ask you to stay here. For the Lord has sent me to the Jordan." And Elisha said, "As the Lord lives and as you yourself live, I will not leave you." So the two of them went on.
7 Now fifty sons of the men who tell what will happen in the future went and stood on the other side of the Jordan River a long way off from the two of them who were standing by the Jordan. 8 Then Elijah took his coat and rolled it up and hit the water. And the water divided to one side and to the other, so the two of them crossed the Jordan on dry ground. 9 When they had crossed, Elijah said to Elisha, "Ask what I should do for you before I am taken from you." And Elisha said, "I ask you, let twice the share of your spirit be upon

me." 10 Elijah said, "You have asked a hard thing. But if you see me when I am taken from you, it will be given to you. But if not, it will not be so." 11 As they went on and talked, a war-wagon of fire and horses of fire came between them. And Elijah went up by a wind-storm to heaven. 12 Elisha saw it and cried out, "My father, my father, the war-wagon of Israel and its horsemen!" And he saw Elijah no more. Then he took hold of his own clothes and tore them in two pieces. 13 He picked up Elijah's coat that had fallen from him. And he returned and stood by the side of the Jordan. 14 He took Elijah's coat that fell from him, and hit the water and said, "Where is the Lord, the God of Elijah?" When he hit the water, it was divided to one side and to the other, and Elisha crossed the Jordan.

15 The sons of the men who tell what will happen in the future at Jericho saw him. And they said, "The spirit of Elijah rests on Elisha." They came to meet him and bowed to the ground in front of him. 16 They said to him, "Now see, there are fifty strong men with your servants. Let them go and look for your teacher. It might be that the Spirit of the Lord has taken him up and put him down on some mountain or into some valley." And Elisha said, "Do not send them." 17 But they talked to him until he was ashamed, and he said, "Send them." So they sent fifty men to look for Elijah. But after three days they did not find him. 18 They returned to Elisha while he was staying at Jericho. And he said to them, "Did I not tell you, 'Do not go'?"

Powerful Works of Elisha

19 Then the men of the city said to Elisha, "See, it is pleasing to live in this city, as my lord sees. But the water is bad. And the land does not bring fruit." 20 Elisha said, "Bring me a new jar, and put salt in it." So they brought it to him. 21 Then he went out to the well of water and threw salt into it,

and said, "This is what the Lord says, 'I have made this water pure. It will not cause death or loss of fruit any more.'" 22 So the water has been pure to this day, just as Elisha said.

23 Then he left there and went to Bethel. On the way, some young boys came out from the city and made fun of him. They said to him, "Go up, you man with no hair! Go up, you man with no hair!" 24 He looked behind him and saw them, and cursed them in the name of the Lord. Then two female bears came from among the trees and tore up forty-two of the boys. 25 Elisha went from there to Mount Carmel, then returned to Samaria.

2 Kings 3

The War between Moab and Israel

3 Ahab's son Jehoram became the king of Israel at Samaria in the eighteenth year of Jehoshaphat king of Judah. He ruled for twelve years. 2 Jehoram did what was bad in the eyes of the Lord, but not like his father and mother. For he put away the object of Baal which his father had made. 3 But he held on to the sins of Jeroboam the son of Nebat, which made Israel sin. He did not leave them.
4 Now Mesha king of Moab raised sheep. He had to pay the king of Israel 100,000 lambs and the wool of 100,000 rams each year. 5 But when Ahab died, the king of Moab turned against the king of Israel. 6 So King Jehoram went out of Samaria at that time and called all Israel together. 7 Then he went and sent word to Jehoshaphat the king of Judah, saying, "The king of Moab has turned against me. Will you go with me to fight against Moab?" And Jehoshaphat said, "I will go. I am as you are. My people are as your people. My horses are as your horses." 8 Then he said, "Which way should we go?" And he answered, "By the way of the desert of Edom." 9 So the king of Israel went with the king of Judah and the king of Edom. They traveled around for seven days, but there was no water for the army or the cattle that followed them. 10 The king of Israel said, "It is bad! For the Lord has called these three kings to give them into the hand of Moab." 11 But Jehoshaphat said, "Is there not a man who speaks for God here? Is there no one we can ask to learn what the Lord would have us do?" One of the servants of the king of Israel answered, "Elisha the son of Shaphat is here. He poured water on the hands of Elijah." 12 And Jehoshaphat said, "The word of the Lord is with

him." So the king of Israel and Jehoshaphat and the king of Edom went down to him.

13 Elisha said to the king of Israel, "What have I to do with you? Go to the men who tell what will happen in the future that your father and mother have gone to." And the king of Israel said to him, "No. It is the Lord Who has called these three kings together to give them into the hand of Moab." 14 Elisha said, "As the Lord of all lives, before Whom I stand, if I did not care for Jehoshaphat the king of Judah, I would not look at you or see you. 15 But now bring me a man who plays music." And when the man played music, the power of the Lord came upon Elisha. 16 He said, "This is what the Lord says, 'Make this valley full of ditches.' 17 For the Lord says, 'You will not see wind or rain. But that valley will be filled with water so that you and your cattle and your animals will drink.' 18 This is only a small thing in the eyes of the Lord. He will give you the Moabites also. 19 Then you will destroy every strong city and cut down every good tree. You will close all the wells of water, and destroy every good piece of land with stones." 20 The next morning, about the time when the gift is given on the altar, water came by the way of Edom. The country was filled with water. 21 Now all the Moabites heard that the kings had come up to fight against them. All who were able to wear battle-clothes, young and old, were called together. And they stood at the side of the land of Moab. 22 They got up early in the morning. The sun was shining on the water. And the Moabites saw that the water beside them was as red as blood. 23 They said, "This is blood. For sure the kings have fought and killed one another. So now, Moab, let us take what is left!" 24 But when they came to the tents of Israel, the Israelites came and fought against the Moabites. The Moabites ran from

them. And Israel went on into the land, killing the Moabites. 25 So they destroyed the cities. Each man threw a stone on every piece of good land until it was covered. They closed all the wells of water and cut down all the good trees. Only the stones of Kir-hareseth were left standing. But the stone-throwers went around it and fought against it. 26 The king of Moab saw that the battle was too hard for him. So he took with him 700 men who used the sword, to break through to the king of Edom. But they could not. 27 Then he took his oldest son who was to rule in his place, and gave him as a burnt gift on the wall. And many became very angry toward Israel. They left him and returned to their own land.

2 Kings 4

Elisha and the Jar of Oil

4 Now the wife of the son of one of the men who tell what will happen in the future cried out to Elisha, "Your servant, my husband, is dead. You know that your servant honored the Lord with fear. But the man to whom he owed money has come to take my two children to make them serve him." 2 Elisha said to her, "What can I do for you? Tell me, what do you have in the house?" And she said, "Your woman servant has nothing in the house except a jar of oil." 3 Then he said, "Go around and get jars from all your neighbors. Get empty jars, many of them. 4 Then go in and shut the door behind you and your sons. Pour the oil into all these jars, and set aside each one that is full." 5 So she went from him and shut the door behind her and her sons. They took the jars to her, and she poured. 6 When the jars were full, she said to her son, "Bring me another jar." And he said to her, "There is not one jar left." Then the oil stopped flowing. 7 She came and told the man of God. And he said, "Go and sell the oil and pay what you owe. You and your sons can live on the rest."

Elisha and the Shunammite's Son

8 One day Elisha went to Shunem. An important woman was there, who talked him into eating some food. So every time he passed by, he would turn in there to eat food. 9 She said to her husband, "Now I see that this is a holy man of God who is always passing by. 10 Let us make a little room on the second floor. And let us put a bed there for him, and a table and a chair and a lamp. Then when he comes to us, he can go in there."

11 One day Elisha came there and went into the room on the second floor, and rested. 12 He said to Gehazi his servant, "Call this Shunammite." When he had called her, she came and stood in front of him. 13 Elisha said to Gehazi, "Now tell her, 'See, you have done much for us. What can I do for you? Should I speak to the king or to the captain of the army for you?'" And she answered, "I live among my own people." 14 So Elisha said, "What then is to be done for her?" Gehazi answered, "She has no son, and her husband is old." 15 Elisha said, "Call her." When he had called her, she stood at the door. 16 Then he said, "At this time next year you will hold a son in your arms." And she said, "No, my lord, O man of God. Do not lie to your woman servant." 17 Later she was going to have a child and she gave birth to a son at that time the next year, as Elisha had told her.

18 When the child was grown, he went out one day to his father who was with those gathering grain. 19 He said to his father, "O, my head, my head!" The father said to his servant, "Carry him to his mother." 20 When he was brought to his mother, he sat on her knees until noon. Then he died. 21 She went up and laid him on the bed of the man of God. She shut the door behind him, and went out. 22 Then she called to her husband and said, "Send me one of the servants and one of the donkeys, that I may run to the man of God and return." 23 Her husband said, "Why will you go to him today? It is not the time of the new moon or the Day of Rest." She said, "It will be all right." 24 Then she put a seat on a donkey and said to her servant, "Drive on. Do not slow down for me unless I tell you." 25 So she went and came to the man of God at Mount Carmel. When the man of God saw her far away, he said to Gehazi his servant, "See, there is the Shunammite. 26 Run now to meet

her. Say to her, 'Is it well with you? Is it well with your husband? Is it well with the child?'" And she answered, "It is well." 27 When she came to the mountain to the man of God, she took hold of his feet. Gehazi came near to push her away, but the man of God said, "Let her alone. For her soul is troubled within her. The Lord has hidden it from me. He has not told me." 28 Then she said, "Did I ask you for a son? Did I not say, 'Do not lie to me'?"

29 Elisha said to Gehazi, "Get ready to travel. Take my walking stick and go. If you meet any man, do not greet him. If anyone greets you, do not answer him. Then lay my stick on the boy's face." 30 The mother of the boy said, "As the Lord lives and as you yourself live, I will not leave you." So Elisha got up and followed her. 31 Gehazi went on before them and laid the stick on the boy's face. But there was no sound or anything to show that the boy was alive. So Gehazi returned to meet Elisha, and told him, "The boy is not awake." 32 When Elisha came into the house, he saw the boy lying dead on his bed. 33 So he went in and shut the door behind the two of them, and prayed to the Lord. 34 He went up and lay on the child. He put his mouth on his mouth, and his eyes on his eyes, and his hands on his hands. He spread himself out on him, and the child's flesh became warm. 35 Then Elisha got up again. He walked from one end of the house to the other. Then he went up and spread himself on the child again. The boy sneezed seven times, and opened his eyes. 36 Elisha called Gehazi and said, "Call this Shunammite." So he called her. When she came to him, he said, "Take up your son." 37 She came and fell at his feet and put her face to the ground. Then she took up her son and went out.

Elisha and the Pot of Food

38 When Elisha returned to Gilgal, there was no food in the land. The sons of the men who tell what will happen in the future were sitting in front of him. Elisha said to his servant, "Put the large pot over the fire and make food ready for the sons of the men who tell what will happen in the future." 39 One of them went out into the field to gather plants. He found a wild vine, and gathered wild gourds from it. He came and cut them up in the pot of food, not knowing what they were. 40 Then they poured it out for the men to eat. As they were eating the food, they cried out, "O man of God, there is death in the pot!" And they could not eat it. 41 But he said, "Get some grain." And he threw it into the pot, and said, "Pour it out for the people to eat." Then there was no danger in the pot.

Elisha Feeds One Hundred Men

42 A man came from Baal-shalishah. He brought the man of God a gift of the first-fruits. There were twenty loaves of barley bread and new-grown grain in his bag. Elisha said, "Give them to the people, that they may eat." 43 But his servant said, "What? Should I put this in front of 100 men?" But Elisha said, "Give them to the people to eat. For the Lord says, 'They will eat and have some left.'" 44 So he put it in front of them. And they ate and had some left, as the word of the Lord had said.

2 Kings 5

Naaman Is Healed

5 Naaman the captain of the army of the king of Syria was an important man to his king. He was much respected, because by him the Lord had made Syria win in battle. Naaman was a strong man of war, but he had a bad skin disease. 2 Now the Syrians had gone out in groups of soldiers, and had taken a little girl from the land of Israel. She served Naaman's wife. 3 And she said to her owner, "I wish that my owner's husband were with the man of God who is in Samaria! Then he would heal his bad skin disease." 4 So Naaman went in and told his king, "This is what the girl from the land of Israel said." 5 The king of Syria said, "Go now, and I will send a letter to the king of Israel." So Naaman went and took with him silver weighing as much as ten men, 6,000 pieces of gold, and ten changes of clothes. 6 He brought the letter to the king of Israel, which said, "I have sent my servant Naaman to you with this letter, that you may heal his bad skin disease." 7 When the king of Israel read the letter, he tore his clothes and said, "Am I God, to kill and to make alive? Is this why this man sends word to me to heal a man's bad skin disease? Think about it. He wants to start a fight with me." 8 Elisha the man of God heard that the king of Israel had torn his clothes. So he sent word to the king, saying, "Why have you torn your clothes? Let him come to me. Then he will know that there is a man of God in Israel." 9 So Naaman came with his horses and his war-wagons, and stood at the door of Elisha's house. 10 Elisha sent a man to him, saying, "Go and wash in the Jordan seven times. And your flesh will be made well and you will be clean." 11 But Naaman was very angry and went away. He said, "I

thought he would come out to me, and stand, and call on the name of the Lord his God. I thought he would wave his hand over the place, and heal the bad skin disease. 12 Are not Abanah and Pharpar, the rivers of Damascus, better than all the waters of Israel? Could I not wash in them and be clean?" So he turned and went away very angry. 13 Then his servants came and said to him, "My father, if the man of God had told you to do some great thing, would you not have done it? How much more then, when he says to you, 'Wash and be clean'?" 14 So Naaman went down into the Jordan River seven times, as the man of God had told him. And his flesh was made as well as the flesh of a little child. He was clean.

15 Then Naaman returned to the man of God with all those who were with him. He came and stood in front of Elisha and said, "See, now I know that there is no God in all the earth but in Israel. So I ask you now to take a gift from your servant." 16 But Elisha said, "As the Lord lives, before Whom I stand, I will take nothing." Naaman tried to talk him into taking it, but he would not. 17 Naaman said, "If not, I ask you, let your servant be given as much dirt as two horses can carry. For your servant will not give burnt gifts or kill animals on the altar in worship to other gods any more. I will only give gifts to the Lord. 18 But may the Lord forgive your servant for this. My king goes into the house of Rimmon to worship there. He rests on my arm and I put my face to the ground in the house of Rimmon. When I put my face to the ground in the house of Rimmon, may the Lord forgive your servant." 19 And Elisha said to him, "Go in peace." So Naaman went away from him a short way.

Gehazi Wants More

20 But Gehazi, the servant of Elisha the man of God, thought, "See, my owner has let Naaman the

Syrian go without receiving the gift he brought. As the Lord lives, I will run after him and take something from him." 21 So Gehazi went after Naaman. When Naaman saw someone running after him, he stepped off the war-wagon to meet him, and said, "Is all well?" 22 Gehazi said, "All is well. My owner has sent me, saying, 'See, just now two young sons of the men who tell what will happen in the future have come to me from the hill country of Ephraim. I ask of you, give them a man's weight in silver and two changes of clothes.'" 23 Naaman said, "Be pleased to take silver weighing as much as two men." And he had him take two bags of silver weighing as much as two men, with two changes of clothes. He gave them to two of his servants. And they carried them before Gehazi. 24 When he came to the hill, Gehazi took them from the servants and put them in the house. Then he sent the men away, and they left. 25 And Gehazi went in and stood in front of his owner. Elisha said to him, "Where have you been, Gehazi?" And he said, "Your servant did not leave." 26 Elisha said to him, "Did I not go with you in spirit when the man turned from his war-wagon to meet you? Was it a time to receive money and clothes and olive fields and grape-fields and sheep and cattle and men servants and women servants? 27 So now the bad skin disease will be upon you and your children forever." And Gehazi went away from Elisha with a bad skin disease. He was as white as snow.

2 Kings 6

The Ax Head That Was Not Lost

6 Now the sons of the men who tell what will happen in the future said to Elisha, "See, the place where we are living under your care is too small for us. 2 Let us go to the Jordan and each of us cut down a tree there. And let us make a place for us to live there." So Elisha said, "Go." 3 Then one of them said, "Be pleased to go with your servants." And Elisha answered, "I will go." 4 So he went with them. When they came to the Jordan, they cut down trees. 5 But as one of them was cutting a tree, the ax head fell into the water. The man cried out, "It is bad, sir! The ax belongs to another man, and I was to return it." 6 The man of God said, "Where did it fall?" And when he showed him the place, Elisha cut off a stick and threw it in, and the iron came to the top of the water. 7 He said, "Pick it up." So his servant put out his hand and took it.

Syrian Army Loses the Battle

8 Now the king of Syria was fighting a war against Israel. He had a meeting with his servants, and said, "This is the place where I will be staying." 9 The man of God sent news to the king of Israel, saying, "Be careful that you do not pass this place. For the Syrians are coming down there." 10 The king of Israel sent men to the place where the man of God said there would be danger. So he saved himself there more than once or twice. 11 The heart of the king of Syria was angry because of this. He called his servants and said to them, "Will you show me which one of us is helping the king of Israel?" 12 And one of his servants said, "None, my lord, O king. Elisha, the man of God who is in Israel, tells the king of Israel the very words you say in your bedroom." 13 So he said, "Go and see

where Elisha is, that I may send men to take him." And he was told, "See, he is in Dothan." 14 So the king of Syria sent horses and war-wagons and an army of many soldiers there. They came during the night and gathered around the city.

15 The servant of the man of God got up early and went out. And he saw an army with horses and war-wagons around the city. The servant said to Elisha, "It is bad, sir! What should we do?" 16 He answered, "Do not be afraid. For those who are with us are more than those who are with them." 17 Then Elisha prayed and said, "O Lord, I pray, open his eyes, that he may see." And the Lord opened the servant's eyes, and he saw. He saw that the mountain was full of horses and war-wagons of fire all around Elisha. 18 When the Syrians came against him, Elisha prayed to the Lord, saying, "Make these people blind, I pray." So the Lord made them blind, as Elisha had said. 19 Then Elisha said to them, "This is not the way. This is not the city. Follow me and I will bring you to the man you are looking for." And he brought them to Samaria.

20 When they had come to Samaria, Elisha said, "O Lord, open the eyes of these men. Let them see." So the Lord opened their eyes, and they saw. They saw they were in the center of Samaria. 21 When the king of Israel saw them, he said to Elisha, "My father, should I kill them? Should I kill them?" 22 He answered, "Do not kill them. Would you kill those you have taken against their will with your sword and bow? Give them bread and water. Let them eat and drink and return to their owner." 23 So he made a big supper for them. When they had eaten and drunk, he sent them away. And they went to their owner. The Syrians sent no more small groups of soldiers into the land of Israel.

Samaria's Trouble

24 After this, Ben-hadad the king of Syria gathered all his army and went up against Samaria. 25 There was a time of no food in Samaria. The Syrian army gathered around it, until a donkey's head sold for eighty pieces of silver. A half cup of dove's waste sold for five pieces of silver. 26 As the king of Israel was passing by on the wall, a woman cried out to him, "Help, my lord, O king!" 27 And he said, "If the Lord does not help you, from where can I help you? From the grain-floor, or from the grape-crusher?" 28 Then the king said to her, "What is your trouble?" And she answered, "This woman said to me, 'Give your son, so we may eat him today. And we will eat my son tomorrow.' 29 So we made my son ready to eat over the fire, and ate him. The next day I said to her, 'Give your son, so we may eat him.' But she has hidden her son." 30 When the king heard the words of the woman, he tore his clothes. He was passing by on the wall, and the people looked. They saw that he wore cloth made from hair under his clothes. 31 Then he said, "May God do so to me and more also, if the head of Elisha the son of Shaphat stays on him today."

32 Now Elisha was sitting in his house. And the leaders were sitting with him. The king sent a man, but before the man came to him, Elisha said to the leaders, "Do you see how this son of a killer has sent to take off my head? See, when the king's man comes, shut the door. Hold the door shut against him. Is not the sound of his owner's feet behind him?" 33 While he was still talking with them, the king came down to him and said, "See, this trouble

is from the Lord. Why should I wait for the Lord
any longer?"

7 Then Elisha said, "Listen to the word of the Lord. The Lord says, 'Tomorrow about this time, a basket of fine flour will be sold for one piece of silver in the gate of Samaria. And two baskets of barley will be sold for a piece of silver.'" 2 The captain on whose arm the king rested said to the man of God, "See, if the Lord should make windows in heaven, could this thing be?" Elisha said, "You will see it with your own eyes. But you will not eat of it."

The Syrians Leave

3 Now there were four men at the city gate with a bad skin disease. They said to one another, "Why do we sit here until we die? 4 If we go into the city, there is no food there and we will die. And if we sit here, we will die also. So now come, let us go over to the tents of the Syrians. If they do not kill us, we will live. And if they kill us, we will die there." 5 So they got up in the evening to go to the Syrians. When they came to the tents of the Syrians, there was no one there. 6 For the Lord had made the Syrian army hear a sound of war-wagons and horses and an army of many soldiers. So they said to one another, "The king of Israel has paid the kings of the Hittites and the kings of the Egyptians to fight against us." 7 And they ran away in the evening. They left their tents and their horses and donkeys. They left everything just as it was, and ran for their lives. 8 Then the men with a bad skin disease came to the tents. They went into one tent and ate and drank. They carried away silver and gold and clothing, and hid them. Then they returned and went into another tent and carried things away from it, and hid them.

9 They said to one another, "We are not doing right. This is a day of good news, but we are keeping quiet. We will be punished if we wait until morning. So now let us go and tell those of the king's house." 10 And they came and called the men who watched the city gate. They said to them, "We went to the tents of the Syrians. But there was no one to be seen or heard there. Only the horses and donkeys were tied there. The tents were left just as they were." 11 So the men at the gate called out, and the news was heard in the king's house. 12 The king got up in the night and said to his servants, "I will tell you what the Syrians have done to us. They know that we are hungry. So they have left the tents to hide themselves in the field. They are saying, 'When they come out of the city, we will take them alive and get into the city.'" 13 One of his servants said, "Let some men take five of the horses that are left. Those who are left in the city are not doing better than all those who have died. So let us send men out to see." 14 So they took two war-wagons with horses. And the king sent them after the Syrian army, saying, "Go and see." 15 They went after them to the Jordan. All the way was covered with clothes and objects which the Syrians had thrown away in their hurry. Then the men returned and told the king.

16 So the people went out and took what the Syrians had left. Then a basket of fine flour was sold for a piece of silver. And two baskets of barley sold for a piece of silver, just as the word of the Lord had said. 17 Now the king chose the captain on whose arm he rested to watch the gate. But the people stepped on him at the gate. He died just as the man of God had said when the king came down to him. 18 It happened just as the man of God had told the king, saying, "About this time tomorrow at the gate of Samaria, two baskets of barley will sell

for a piece of silver. And a basket of fine flour will sell for a piece of silver." 19 Then the captain had said to the man of God, "See, if the Lord should make windows in heaven, could such a thing be?" And Elisha had said, "You will see it with your own eyes. But you will not eat of it." 20 So it happened to him. The people stepped on him at the gate, and he died.

2 Kings 8

The Shunammite's Land Given Back

8 Now Elisha spoke to the woman whose son he had brought back to life. He said, "Get ready and go with those of your house. Stay in whatever country you can. For the Lord has called for a time of no food. It will come upon the land for seven years." 2 So the woman got ready as the man of God had told her. She went with those of her house and stayed in the land of the Philistines seven years. 3 At the end of seven years she returned from the land of the Philistines. And she went out to ask the king for her house and field. 4 Now the king was talking with Gehazi, the servant of the man of God, saying, "Tell me all the great things that Elisha has done." 5 Gehazi started telling the king how Elisha had brought the one who was dead to life again. Then the woman whose son he had brought back to life asked the king for her house and field. And Gehazi said, "My lord, O king, this is the woman and this is her son, whom Elisha brought back to life." 6 When the king asked the woman, she told him what had happened. So the king chose a certain captain to help her, saying, "Give her all that was hers. And give her all the food taken from the field from the day she left the land until now."

The Death of Ben-hadad

7 Then Elisha came to Damascus. Ben-hadad the king of Syria was sick, and he was told, "The man of God has come here." 8 The king said to Hazael, "Take a gift and go meet the man of God. Ask the Lord through him, saying, 'Will I get better from this sickness?'" 9 So Hazael went to meet Elisha and took with him a gift of every kind of good thing of Damascus. It took forty camels to carry it all. He came and stood in front of Elisha and said, "Your

son Ben-hadad king of Syria has sent me to you, saying, 'Will I get better from this sickness?'" 10 Elisha said to him, "Go and tell him, 'You will get better for sure.' But the Lord has shown me that he will die for sure." 11 Then Elisha looked at Hazael until he was ashamed. And the man of God cried. 12 Hazael said, "Why are you crying, my lord?" Then Elisha answered, "Because I know the bad things that you will do to the people of Israel. You will set their strong places on fire. You will kill their young men with the sword. You will crush their little ones against the stones. And you will cut up their women who are with child." 13 Hazael said, "What is your servant, only a dog, that he should do this bad thing?" Elisha answered, "The Lord has shown me that you will be the king of Syria." 14 Then he left Elisha and returned to his owner. Ben-hadad said to him, "What did Elisha tell you?" And Hazael answered, "He told me that you will get better for sure." 15 But the next day Hazael took the bed covering and put it in water. Then he spread it on Ben-hadad's face so that he died. And Hazael became king in his place.

Jehoram Rules Judah

16 In the fifth year of Joram the son of Ahab, king of Israel, Jehoram the son of Jehoshaphat king of Judah began to rule. 17 He was thirty-two years old when he became king. He ruled eight years in Jerusalem. 18 He walked in the way of the kings of Israel, just as those of Ahab's house had done. Ahab's daughter became his wife. He did what was sinful in the eyes of the Lord. 19 But the Lord was not willing to destroy Judah, because of His servant David. The Lord had promised to give David one to rule through his sons always.

20 In his days Edom turned against the rule of Judah and chose a king of their own. 21 Then Joram crossed over to Zair, with all his war-wagons. He and his war-wagon captains got up during the night and fought against the Edomites who had gathered around them. But his army ran away to their tents. 22 So Edom turned against the rule of Judah to this day. Libnah turned against Judah's rule at the same time. 23 The rest of the acts of Joram and all he did, are they not written in the Book of Chronicles of the Kings of Judah? 24 Then Joram died and was buried in the city of David. His son Ahaziah became king in his place.

Ahaziah Rules Judah

25 In the twelfth year of Ahab's son Joram the king of Israel, Ahaziah the son of Jehoram king of Judah began to rule. 26 Ahaziah was twenty-two years old when he became king. He ruled one year in Jerusalem. His mother's name was Athaliah the granddaughter of Omri king of Israel. 27 He walked in the way of the family of Ahab. He did what was sinful in the eyes of the Lord, like those of the family of Ahab had done, because he was a son-in-law of the family of Ahab. 28 He went with Ahab's son Joram to war against Hazael king of Syria at Ramoth-gilead. And the Syrians hurt Joram. 29 So King Joram returned to Jezreel to be healed of the cuts the Syrians had given him at Ramah when he fought against Hazael king of Syria. Then Jehoram's son Ahaziah king of Judah went down to Jezreel to see Joram the son of Ahab because he was sick.

2 Kings 9

Jehu Is Chosen to Be King of Israel

9 Now Elisha the man of God called one of the sons of those who spoke for God. He said to him, "Get ready to travel. Take this jar of oil and go to Ramoth-gilead. 2 When you get there, find Jehu the son of Jehoshaphat son of Nimshi. Go in and have him come away from his brothers. Bring him into a room in the house. 3 Then take the jar of oil and pour it on his head and say, 'The Lord says, "I have chosen you to be the king of Israel."'' Then open the door and run. Do not wait." 4 So the young servant of the man of God went to Ramoth-gilead. 5 When he came, he found the captains of the army sitting there. He said, "I have something to tell you, O captain." And Jehu said, "Which one of us?" And he said, "You, O captain." 6 So he got up and went into the house. He poured the oil on Jehu's head and said to him, "The Lord, the God of Israel, says, 'I have chosen you king over the people of the Lord, over Israel. 7 You are to destroy the house of your owner Ahab, so that I will punish Jezebel for the blood of My servants who speak for God, and the blood of all the Lord's servants. 8 The whole family of Ahab must be destroyed. And I will destroy every male person in Israel who belongs to Ahab, both the servants and those who are free. 9 I will make the family of Ahab like the family of Jeroboam the son of Nebat, and like the family of Baasha the son of Ahijah. 10 The dogs will eat Jezebel in the land of Jezreel. No one will bury her.'" Then he opened the door and ran away.
11 When Jehu came out to his owner's servants, one said to him, "Is all well? Why did this crazy person come to you?" Jehu said, "You know the man and his talk." 12 And they said, "That is not true. Tell us

now." Jehu said, "This is how he spoke to me. He said, 'The Lord says, "I have chosen you to be the king of Israel."'" 13 Then each man took his clothes in a hurry and put them under him on the steps. And they sounded the horn and said, "Jehu is king!"

Joram of Israel Is Killed

14 So Jehu the son of Jehoshaphat the son of Nimshi made plans against Joram. Now Joram and all Israel were fighting against Hazael king of Syria at Ramoth-gilead. 15 But King Joram had returned to Jezreel to be healed of the cuts the Syrians had given him, when he fought with King Hazael of Syria. So Jehu said, "If this is what you have in mind, then let no one get out of the city to tell the news in Jezreel." 16 Then Jehu went to Jezreel in a war-wagon, for Joram was lying there. And Ahaziah the king of Judah had come down to see Joram.
17 Now the man who watched for danger was standing in the tower in Jezreel. He saw the group of Jehu's men coming, and said, "I see a group of men coming." Joram said, "Send a horseman to meet them and ask, 'Do you come in peace?'" 18 So a horseman went to meet him and said, "The king asks, 'Do you come in peace?'" And Jehu said, "What have you to do with peace? Get behind me." Then the watchman told Joram, "The horseman came to them, but he did not return." 19 So he sent out a second horseman, who came to them and said, "The king asks, 'Do you come in peace?'" And Jehu answered, "What have you to do with peace? Get behind me." 20 The watchman told Joram, "He came to them, and he did not return. The leader goes in his war-wagon like a mad man, just like Jehu."

21 Then Joram said, "Get ready." And they made his war-wagon ready. Then Joram king of Israel and Ahaziah king of Judah went out, each in their war-wagon, to meet Jehu. They found him in the field of Naboth the Jezreelite. 22 When Joram saw Jehu, he said, "Do you come in peace, Jehu?" And he answered, "What peace can there be, so long as the sinful ways and witchcrafts of your mother Jezebel are so many?" 23 So Joram turned the horses around and ran away, saying to Ahaziah, "He is turning against the king, O Ahaziah!" 24 Jehu pulled his bow with all his strength and shot Joram between his arms. The arrow went through his heart, and he fell in his war-wagon. 25 Then Jehu said to Bidkar his captain, "Pick him up and throw him into the field of Naboth the Jezreelite. For I remember when you and I were going together after his father Ahab. The Lord said then that this would happen to him. 26 The Lord said, 'Yesterday I have seen the blood of Naboth and his sons. I will punish you in this field.' So now take and throw him into the field, as the word of the Lord has said."

Ahaziah of Judah Is Killed

27 When Ahaziah the king of Judah saw this, he ran away toward the garden house. Jehu went after him and said, "Shoot him in the war-wagon also." So they shot him at the hill of Gur, by Ibleam. But he got away to Megiddo and died there. 28 His servants carried him in a war-wagon to Jerusalem. They buried him in his grave with his fathers in the city of David.
29 In the eleventh year of Joram the son of Ahab, Ahaziah became the king of Judah.

Queen Jezebel Is Killed

30 When Jehu came to Jezreel, Jezebel heard about it. She colored her eyes and combed her hair, and then looked out the window. 31 As Jehu came through the gate, she said, "Is it well, Zimri, your owner's killer?" 32 Then he looked up to the window and said, "Who is on my side? Who?" And two or three men looked down at him. 33 Then he said, "Throw her down." So they threw Jezebel down. Some of her blood went on the wall and on the horses. And Jehu made his war-wagons go over her. 34 Then Jehu went in and ate and drank. And he said, "Now go out to this sinful woman and bury her, for she is a king's daughter." 35 So they went to bury her. But all they found were her skull and feet and hands. 36 When they returned and told Jehu, he said, "This is the word of the Lord, which He spoke by His servant Elijah the Tishbite. He said, 'In the land of Jezreel the dogs will eat the flesh of Jezebel. 37 Jezebel's body will be as waste on the field in the land of Jezreel. So no one will be able to say, "This is Jezebel."'"

43

Title:

Text:

Theme:

45

I.____

II.______________________________________

III.______________________________________

Take Away:

Title:

Text:

Theme:

I.____

II.____

III.____

Take Away:

Title:

Text:

Theme:

47

I.____

II.____

III.____

Take Away:

Title:

Text:

Theme:

I.______________________________________

II.______________________________________

III.______________________________________

Take Away:

Title:

Text:

Theme:

49

I.______________________________________

II.______________________________________

III.______________________________________

Take Away:

Title:

Text:

Theme:

50

I.____

II.____

III.____

Take Away:

Title:

Text:

Theme:

51

I.____

II.____

III.______________________________________

Take Away:

Title:

Text:

Theme:

52

I.____

II.____

III.____

Take Away:

Title:

Text:

Theme:

53

I.______________________________________

II.______________________________________

III.______________________________________

Take Away:

Title:

Text:

Theme:

54

I.______________________________________

II.______________________________________

III.______________________________________

Take Away:

Title:

Text:

Theme:

55

I.______________________________________

II.______________________________________

III.______________________________________

Take Away:

55

Title:

Text:

Theme:

56

I.____

II.____

III.____

Take Away:

Title:

Text:

Theme:

57

I.____

II.____

III.____

Take Away:

Title:

Text:

Theme:

58

I.___________________________________

II.___________________________________

III.___________________________________

Take Away:

Title:

Text:

Theme:

I.____

II.____

III.____

Take Away:

Title:

Text:

Theme:

60

I.____

II.____

III.____

Take Away:

Title:

Text:

Theme:

I.______________________________________

II._____________________________________

III.____________________________________

Take Away:

Title:

Text:

Theme:

62

I.______________________________________

II.______________________________________

III.______________________________________

Take Away:

Title:

Text:

Theme:

63

I. ____

II. ____

III. ____

Take Away:

Title:

Text:

Theme:

I.______________________________________

II.______________________________________

III.______________________________________

Take Away:

Title:

Text:

Theme:

65

I.____

II.____

III.____

Take Away:

Title:

Text:

Theme:

66

I.______________________________

II.______________________________

III.______________________________

Take Away:

Title:

Text:

Theme:

I.____

II.____

III.____

Take Away:

Title:

Text:

Theme:

I.____

II.____

III.____

Take Away:

Title:

Text:

Theme:

I.____

II.____

III.____

Take Away:

Title:

Text:

Theme:

I.____

II.____

III.____

Take Away:

Title:

Text:

Theme:

71

I.______________________________

II.______________________________

III.______________________________

Take Away:

Title:

Text:

Theme:

I.____________________________________

II.____________________________________

III.____________________________________

Take Away:

Title:

Text:

Theme:

73

I.____

II.____

III.____

Take Away:

Title:

Text:

Theme:

74

I.____

II.____

III.____

Take Away:

Title:

Text:

Theme:

75

I.____

II.____

III.____

Take Away:

Title:

Text:

Theme:

I.______________________________________

II.______________________________________

III.______________________________________

Take Away:

Title:

Text:

Theme:

I.____

II.____

III.____

Take Away:

Title:

Text:

Theme:

I.______________________________________

II.______________________________________

III.______________________________________

Take Away:

Title:

Text:

Theme:

I.______________________________________

II.______________________________________

III.______________________________________

Take Away:

Title:

Text:

Theme:

80

I.____

II.____

III.____

Take Away:

Title:

Text:

Theme:

I.______________________________________

II.______________________________________

III.______________________________________

Take Away:

Title:

Text:

Theme:

82

I.____

II.____

III.____

Take Away:

Title:

Text:

Theme:

I._______________________________________

II._______________________________________

III._______________________________________

Take Away:

Title:

Text:

Theme:

84

I.____

II.____

III.____

Take Away:

84

Title:

Text:

Theme:

85

I.____

II.____

III.____

Take Away:

Title:

Text:

Theme:

I.____

II.____

III.____

Take Away:

Title:

Text:

Theme:

87

I.______________________________________

II.______________________________________

III.______________________________________

Take Away:

Title:

Text:

Theme:

I.____

II.____

III.____

Take Away:

Title:

Text:

Theme:

I.____

II.____

III.____

Take Away:

Title:

Text:

Theme:

90

I.____

II.____

III.____

Take Away:

Title:

Text:

Theme:

91

I.____

II.____

III.____

Take Away:

Title:

Text:

Theme:

92

I.____

II.____

III.____

Take Away:

9 7 9 8 7 0 6 5 3 9 6 7 2